12 Financial Stories for Muslim Kids

Mansoor Limba

ISBN: 9798782391935

DEDICATION

Dedicated to all parents.

CONTENTS

PREFACE

I begin in the Name of God, the Most Kind, the Most Merciful.

It was then my daughter's first summer vacation after graduation in elementary. Over lunch I was mentioning to her the articles I was planning to post at one of my blogs – www.MuslimandMoney.com – and also the book – 'Muslim Couple and Money' – I was currently writing then.

Curious enough, she asked, "Papa, do you have also plan to write 'Muslim Kid and Money' for us youngsters?"

Almost spontaneously, I replied, "Yes, I also want to… Can you help me in this project?"

"How?"

"In your spare time, read short stories and then select 12 stories you like most. And then I am going to edit the stories and give some annotations or explanations."

"How should I select?"

"Do you mean the criteria for selection?"

"Yes."

"You select the 12 stories whose moral lessons in personal financial literary and behavioral economics you like most."

"Papa, what do you mean by 'behavioral economics'?"

(Expectedly, she no longer asked about personal finance or financial literacy, as she has already some ideas about it due to our many earlier conversations – especially during meals.)

"Behavioral economics is simply a method of economic analysis that applies psychological insights why people make economic decisions – buying, selling, consuming products and services, etc. – the way they do."

"Okay!"

Fast forward: the book in your hand is the said father-daughter joint project.

Why did I edit this book, by the way?

I edited this book because:

* Financial literary must begin at childhood.

* Financial literary is something that children do not learn in school, do they?

* Storytelling is one of the best ways to impart moral lessons to children. And who doesn't want to be told by his mother or grandmother wonderful stories during bedtime?

So, is there any better way to impart this learning to our children than storytelling?

At the end of each story, there is a concise explanation of financial lessons the young reader can learn.

Among these lessons are:

* The importance of right attitude in assuring one's financial success;

* The amount of income one gets is immaterial if there is no discipline in spending;

* How much you save is not that important, but rather the cultivation of the habit of saving;

* It is not enough that extra money is saved; it must be

invested as well; in other words, apart from setting it aside, it must be allowed to work in order to multiply;

* The greatest investment is investment in one's own self – how to make yourself more productive and profitable.

Is the book solely intended for Muslim kids?

No.

The stories will be interesting not only to Muslims but also non-Muslim kids as well. It is "for Muslim kids" simply because most of the stories are in a Muslim cultural setting, but the moral lessons imparted in each story is universal and beneficial to all youngsters irrespective of religious affiliations or ideological persuasions.

In order to attract the attention and interest of the intended readers, this book uses children-friendly fonts and is written in an easy-to-understand language.

If you want your child to grow up as financial responsible, then what are you waiting for?

Enjoy reading!

****

STORY 1
YUSUF THE NATIONAL TREASURER

Yusuf (Joseph) (*'alayhis-salām* – on whom be peace) was one of the prophets (*anbiya'*) mentioned in the Qur'an. His father, Ya'qub (Jacob) (*'alayhis-salām* – on whom be peace) was also a prophet (*nabi*). He had eleven brothers. Ten were older than him, and one was younger, Benyamin (Benjamin).

Being a very good and handsome boy and loved by his father very much, Yusuf earned the jealousy of his ten older brothers. So, they decided to get rid of him when he reached the age of 17.

Once Yusuf said to his father, "O father, I saw eleven planets and the sun and the moon, prostrating before me." (Qur'an 12:4)

He said, "O my son, do not mention your

dream to your brothers, lest they become jealous of you." (Qur'an 12:5)

One day the ten older brothers convince their father to bring Yusuf with them in the field where they threw him in a well and sold him as a slave to a caravan.

Yusuf was sold in the marketplace of Egypt to a man and his wife, who had no children of their own.

The man was an Egyptian, an officer of Fir'awn (Pharaoh), the King of Egypt. His wife's name was Zulaykha.

Under their custodianship, Yusuf grew up as a handsome and good-looking man, and God endowed him with wisdom and knowledge. (Qur'an 12:22)

After sometime, his master's wife tried to seduce him, which he naturally refused. As they raced toward the door, she grabbed and tore his shirt from behind, and they found her husband by the door. When he saw that his shirt was torn from the back he said to her:

"This is a device on your part, and the women's deceit is mighty indeed. As for you Yusuf, you can forget the whole thing. As you my wife, ask forgiveness for your sin. You are certainly wrong." (Qur'an 12:28-29)

Some women in the city gossiped: "The governor's wife is trying to seduce her servant. She is madly in love with him. What she is doing is really error." (Qur'an 12:30)

When she heard of their gossip, she sent for them and prepared a feast. After she gave each one of them a knife, she said to him (Yusuf): "Go out to them!"

When they saw him, they so admired him that they cut their hands and said: "By God, this is not a human being, he is a handsome angel." (Qur'an 12:31)

She said, "This is the one about whom you blame me, I did try to seduce him, he refused. Unless he does what I command him to do, he will be imprisoned, and debased." (Qur'an 12:32)

He said, "My Lord, the prison is better for me than what they invite me to do, unless you divert their evil from me. I may desire them and behave like the ignorant." (Qur'an 12:33)

As answer to his prayer, they later decided, in spite of all the sign, to imprison him for awhile. (Qur'an 12:35)

Two young men entered the prison with him. One of them said, "I saw myself in a dream pressing wine."

The other one said, "I saw myself carrying

bread on my head from which the birds were eating." (Qur'an 12:36)

As he was guided to the right path, before interpreting the dreams, Yusuf preached his religion to two of his companions in prison. He said, "I have been telling you of every food that came to you as provision, even before it came to you. That is what my Lord has taught me, for I have forsaken the religion of people who disbelieve in God and the hereafter." (Qur'an 12:37)

He also said, "O my prison companions! One of you will be the king's wine butler. As for the other, he will be crucified, and the birds will eat from his head. This is the opinion concerning your inquiry." (Qur'an 12:41)

He then said to the one to be saved, "Remember me in your master's presence."

But Yusuf's companion went out of prison, he forgot to remember him in the presence of the King, and Yusuf remained in prison a few more years. (Qur'an 12:42)

Years later while Yusuf was in prison, the Fir'awn of Egypt had a dream which caused him much concern.

The King said, "I saw seven fat cows being eaten by seven thin cows; and seven green ears of wheat, and seven dried ones. O you elders, explain my dream to me if you can interpret the dream the dreams."

They said, "This is probably a nonsense dream. We know nothing about the interpretation of dreams."

Then the one who had been saved remembered after such a long time and said, "I tell you the interpretation thereof if you send me to Yusuf!" (Qur'an 12:45)

As he was sent to the prison, he said, "Yusuf, my friend, explain to us seven fat cows being eaten by seven thin cows, and seven green ears of wheat, and seven dried ones, that I may return to the people, and let them know." (Qur'an 12:46)

Yusuf explained, "The dream means that the first seven years to come will be good years with good harvest, but the next seven years to follow will be bad years with famine and hunger."

He then continued, "You will produce good crops for seven conservative years. When you harvest, you should store them in their ears, except for a minimum that you eat." (Qur'an 12:47)

Yusuf also said, "Then seven bad years will

follow, and will exhaust what you had advanced for them, except for a little that may be left. After that, a year will come in which the people will prosper, and will again press (wine and oil). (Qur'an 12:48-49)

The King said, "Bring him to me!"

When the messenger went to him, Yusuf said, "Go back to your master and ask him about the women who cut their hands. My Lord is fully aware of their schemes." (Qur'an 12:50)

The King said, "What happened when you tried to seduce Yusuf?"

They said, "God forbid, we have not known of anything bad about him."

The governor's wife said, "Now the truth is manifest. I am the one who tried to seduce him. He had told the truth. Now he should know that I did not betray him in his absence. God does not bless the schemes of the betrayers." (Qur'an 12:51-52)

She continued, "I claim no innocence for myself. Surely, the self advocates evil, except for those blessed by my Lord. My Lord is forgiver, merciful." (Qur'an 12:53)

The King said, "Bring him to me, to have him work for me."

When the King talked to Yusuf, he said, "As

of now, you are our trusted confidant." (Qur'an 12:54)

Yusuf said, "Put me in charge of the treasury. I am an experienced treasurer." (Qur'an 12:55)

The King made him the treasurer and inspector of Egypt's storage chambers.

At that time, Yusuf was thirty years old.

After the King appointed him treasurer, Yusuf married the governor's wife who became widow.

Not long after that, Yusuf met and forgave his ten brothers who betrayed and sold him as a slave. He was also reunited with his father Ya'qub and younger brother Benyamin, and he invited his whole family to live in Egypt. (Qur'an 12:100-101)

God establish Yusuf in the land of Egypt, ruling therein as he pleased. God endowed him with mercy, and He never neglected to reward the righteous. (Qur'an 12:56)

Source: Iljas Ismail, STORIES OF TWENTY FIVE PROPHETS MENTIONED IN THE HOLY QUR'AN, Story 10.

Financial Lessons of the Story:

1. Trust in God (*tawakkal 'alallah*) at all times.

2. Preservation of one's self-esteem and personal integrity.

3. Utilization of one's energy and talent to earn for a living.

4. Identification of one's niche – what one can do best and passionate of;

5. Maintenance of one's network of friends, co-workers, and relatives.

6. Importance of saving in facing any emergency in the future.

****

STORY 2
A MAN WHO ASKED FOR HELP

Reviewing his own painful past full of afflictions, he recalled how the bitter days slipped away, the days he was not even in a position to provide the daily meals for his wife and innocent children. He laid musingly on how a few words, which had pricked up his ears for three times and animated his spirit, deviated the course of his life, and rescued his whole family from poverty and calamity overwhelming them.

He was one of the Holy Prophet's Companions; poverty and indigence had upper hand on him.

One day amicably reaching the dead end, after consulting with his family, he decided to go to the Holy Prophet (peace be upon him and his family), what his wife had suggested, to expose his situation and ask him for financial assistance. With this intention he came out of his house, yet did he not offer his request, the following words fell upon his ears:

"We help whoever demands us for assistance, but Allah preserves the needs of those who feel enriched and refrained from stretching out their hands before someone else."

He returned back home without uttering a single word. He found himself again to face the awful silhouette of the poverty overshadowing his dwelling place. The next day, he rejoined compulsively the assembly of the Holy Prophet with the same intention. He heard the same words from the Holy Prophet:

"We help whoever demands us for assistance, but Allah preserves the needs of those who feel enriched and refrained from stretching out their hands before someone else."

He returned home once again without putting forward his request. For the third time, he saw himself indulging in the jungle of poverty, debility, misery, and helplessness; he decided to go to the assembly of the Holy

Prophet in order to put forward his intention. Once again the lips of the Prophet moved and the same words were repeated, invigorating the heart and giving certainty to the spirit.

This time, by hearing those words, the man felt more confidence and perceived that he had found the key of his problem. He went out with more assured steps, thinking: "I will never ask for someone's help. I will rely on Allah and take advantage of the energy and the capacity which exists in my own self, and I will pray to Him to make me succeed in what I will undertake to do and enrich me."

He thought what kind of job would be suitable for him to look for. In such circumstances, he decided to go to the desert, gather some firewood and sell them. He went and borrowed an ax, then he left for desert. By gathering the firewood and selling it, he relished the result of his own toil. He continued working hard for the following days until he managed to buy an ax, a beast of burden, and the other means of work with the gained money. He continued working till he gained a capital and owned the servants. One day the Holy Prophet met him. While having the smile on his lips, he said:

"We will help whoever demands us, but Allah preserves the needs of those who feel free from want." (*Usul al-Kafi*, vol. 2, p. 139 (*Al-Qina'a*); *Safinat al-Bihar* (*Qana'a*).)

Source: Murtada Mutahhari, THE NARRATIVES OF THE VERACIOUS, Story 2.

Financial Lessons of the Story:
1. Trust in God (*tawakkal 'alallah*) at all times.
2. Preservation of one's self-esteem and personal integrity.
3. Utilization of one's energy and talent to earn for a living.
4. Identification of one's niche – what one can do best and passionate of.
5. Investing in things that would further earn income – "an ax, a beast of burden and the other means of work."
6. Looking for livelihood for one's family in order not to depend on others is a form of worship (*'ibadah*).

****

STORY 3
TYING THE KNEES OF CAMEL

The caravan being tramped for hours, tiredness overwhelmed the riders and the animals. As soon as they reached an oasis where there was water, they had their camels kneel down. The Holy Prophet, accompanying the caravan, made his camel kneel down and dismounted from it. All were rushing to reach the water to prepare for the preliminaries of prayer. Dismounting from the camel, the Holy Prophet also made his way towards the water.

After covering a certain distance, without speaking to anyone, he returned back to his camel. To the surprise of his Companions, they thought he was not pleased with this place and will order them to set out?! Lending the ears to him, in full attention, they looked forward to hear his order. The Companions were astonished and amazed when they saw the Holy Prophet reach his camel, pick up tie and bind the knees of it; then he returned back towards his first destination.

The exclamation rose up in between the Companions: "O Messenger of Allah! Why did you not command us to do that, and you bothered yourself while we are all proud of being at your service?"

The Holy Prophet replied: "Do not ever ask for help from others for your own affairs and do not count upon others even if it would be a toothpick." (*Kahl al-Bassar*, p. 69)

Source: Murtada Mutahhari, THE NARRATIVES OF THE VERACIOUS, Story 4.

Financial Lessons of the Story:
1. To be self-reliant and not to rely on others even for a small thing.
2. Preservation of one's self-esteem and personal integrity.

****

STORY 4
A COMPANION OF HAJJ PILGRIMAGE

On returning from journey of Hajj pilgrimage, a man related his and his Companions' experience who accompanied him, to Imam Ja'far al-Sadiq, a great grandson of Prophet Muhammad. He stirred and admired them, particularly one of his fellow-travelers: "How noble was he. We are proud of accompanying such an honorable man. He was praying continuously. No sooner did we stop at a place immediately than he would part from us, seek a corner, spread his prayer mat, and engage himself in prayer and worship.

The Imam asked: "Then, who was looking after his affairs? And who was tending his animal?"

He replied: "Of course, we were. We had the honor to be at his service. He had nothing to worry about; he used to engage himself in his holy affairs."

The Imam replied: "Therefore all of you were better than him."

Source: Murtada Mutahhari, THE NARRATIVES OF THE VERACIOUS, Story 5.

Financial Lessons of the Story:

1. To be self-reliant and not to rely on others even for a small thing.

2. To engage in worship cannot be an excuse to abandon one's physical necessities and social obligations.

3. Looking for livelihood for one's family in order not to depend on others is a form of worship (*'ibadah*).

****

STORY 5
'ALI AND ASSEM

After the end of the battle of Jamal, Imam 'Ali ibn Abi Talib arrived in Basrah. During his stay in Basrah, once he went to visit one of his companions named 'Ala ibn Ziyad Harithi. This man owned a very big and luxurious residence with all comforts. 'Ali, after traversing his eyes on such big and magnificent building, said: "What is the use of such big residence in this world while you are in more need of a vast abode in the hereafter? If you wish to make use of it as a means to attain a spacious residence in the hereafter, you must welcome and entertain guests, be friendly with your blood relatives, clarify the rights of Muslims, take an advantage to vitalize and reveal the rights of others and neglect your personal greedy monopoly and individuality in its use."

'Ala said: "O Leader of the believers! I complain to you of my brother, Assem."

Imam 'Ali: "What is the complaint?"

'Ala: "He has started the life of a recluse, dressed himself in rags, isolated himself from this world, and deserted everything and everyone."

Imam 'Ali: "Bring him in front of me!"

Assem was brought before the Imam, who turned the face towards him and said: "O enemy of your own life! The devil has stolen your sense. Why don't you have sympathy for your wife and children? Do you believe that Allah, Who made the pure bounties of life licit for you, will be displeased with you if you benefit them? You are smaller than that before Allah."

Assem: "O Leader of the believers! You are also like me, imposing the difficulties on yourself! You do not cover your body with soft dresses, nor eat delicious meals. Therefore, I am doing the same thing which you are doing, and I am following the same path which you have chosen."

Imam 'Ali: "You are making a mistake. There is difference between you and me. I shoulder responsibilities of Leadership of Government, but you do not. The duties of a Leader and Governor are something else. Allah made incumbent on the just leaders to take the weakest social classes of people as an example of their own personal lives and live in the same manner as the most empty-handed ones survived so that poverty and indigency does not leave impression on them. Therefore, I am having responsibilities and you have another obligation." (*Nahj al-Balaghah*, Sermon 208)

Source: Murtada Mutahhari, THE NARRATIVES OF THE VERACIOUS, Story 16.

Financial Lessons of the Story:

1. To engage in worship cannot be an excuse to abandon one's physical necessities and social obligations.

2. Both attachment to material things and abandonment of the good things in this world are condemnable in Islam.

3. The Leader is supposed to serve as a model and to consider the condition of the lowest class in society.

4. Looking for livelihood for one's family in order not to depend on others is a form of worship (*'ibadah*).

****

STORY 6
THE NEEDY AND THE WEALTHY

As usual, the Holy Prophet was sitting in his place in between his Companions. They formed a circle around him, *and it seemed to be as if the Prophet was a bezel of a ring in between them.*

Suddenly one of the Muslims, a poor man dressed in rags, came in through the door. According to the Islamic tradition, regardless of his status, anyone who enters in an assembly should sit wherever he finds an empty place, not considering whether the particular place is suitable for his social status. Therefore, that man looked around, found a vacant place, went, and sat there.

Incidentally he settled down next to a rich and wealthy man. The rich man gathered the edges of his dress and shifted on to another side away from him.

The Holy Prophet was watching and observing the behavior of the wealthy person.

He turned towards him and said: "Are you afraid that something of his poverty would transfer to you?"

"No, O Messenger of Allah!"

"Did you fear that some of your wealth might adhere to him?"

"No, O Messenger of Allah!"

"Perhaps..."

"No, O Messenger of Allah!"

"Then why did you draw yourself aside and shift away from him?"

"I confess that I committed an error and made a mistake. At present, in order to compensate my error and to expiate the sin, I am ready to grant half of my wealth to this Muslim brother towards whom I have shown disrespect."

The man in rags replied: "But I am not ready to accept this offer."

The Companions asked: "Why?"

The man said: "I fear that I may become arrogant and ill-treat one of my Muslim brothers in the same way that this man did towards me today."

Source: Murtada Mutahhari, THE NARRATIVES OF THE VERACIOUS, Story 17.

Financial Lesson of the Story:

1. Preservation of one's self-esteem and personal integrity under whatever financial condition.

****

STORY 7
ASCETIC'S ADVICE

The summer heat had become intensified. The sun rays beat down Madinah"s city, garden and farms around it. In such a critical weather condition, a man named Muhammad ibn Munkadar – identified himself as one of the ascetics, pious and anchorites – arrived in Madinah. His eyes cast over a corpulent man who had obviously come out to visit and inspect his farms at that time. Because of his fatness and tiredness, he was treading by his side with the help of a few persons, certainly his friends and relatives.

He thought: "Who is this man in this hot weather of the day leading a busy worldly life?" He came nearer to this person. To his surprise, he was Imam Muhammad ibn 'Ali ibn al-Husayn

(Imam al-Baqir), a great grandson of the Holy Prophet!

He thought: "Why does this noble man indulge in this world?! I must give him an advice and dissuade him from this way!" He came forward and greet the Imam.

Imam Muhammad al-Baqir, out of breath, sweating, returned his greetings.

He said: "Is it suitable for such an honorable personality like you to come out at this hour of the day and in such a hot weather in order to indulge in this world, particularly, with this stoutness which certainly makes you suffer much?"

He continued, "Who is informed of death? Who knows when he will die? The death might overcome you right now; may Allah protect! For instance if death overtakes you in such a condition, what would be your destiny? It is not worthy of you to be after the world, endure so much pain, and suffer with this fat body in these hot days! No! No! It is not worthy of you!"

Imam al-Baqir, removing his hands from his men's shoulders, leaning against the wall and said: "If death overtakes me just now, and I die, I will leave this world while I am performing my duties and worshiping Allah.

Regarding this work, it is just like obedience and submission to Allah. You have imagined that worship is confined to invocation, prayers, and supplication. I have to live and maintain my family. If I do not work nor endure pain, I will have to stretch out my hands towards you or people like you to help me out. I am working for livelihood so that I may not be in need of any person. I must be afraid of my death when I have committed sins, violated and disobeyed the Divine Commandments and not in such a state of obedience to the Orders of Allah, the Almighty, Who has ordered me not to be burden to others, but rather, to gain my own daily bread."

The ascetic said: "I made a big mistake! I thought that I would make an advice to guide others, but now, I have come to understand that I had been mistaken and that I was following a wrong way and was totally in need of advice myself."

Source: Murtada Mutahhari, THE NARRATIVES OF THE VERACIOUS, Story 21.

Financial Lessons of the Story:

1. To be self-reliant and not to rely on others even for a small thing.

2. To engage in worship cannot be an excuse to abandon one's physical necessities and social obligations.

3. Both attachment to material things and abandonment of the good things in this world are condemnable in Islam.

4. Looking for livelihood for one's family in order not to depend on others is a form of worship (*'ibadah*).

****

STORY 8
THE BLACK MARKET

The family of Imam Ja'far al-Sadiq, a great grandson of Prophet Muhammad, increased in number. And so did the cost of living. The Imam decided to do trading to increase his income through investing capital so as to meet his family expenses. He arranged an amount of one thousand Dinars and told his servant Musaddif to take that amount of one thousand Dinars and get ready for a trade journey to Egypt.

Musaddif, with that money went and purchased a type of goods usually exported to Egypt. He went and joined with a caravan of traders who were taking the same type of merchandise to Egypt and left for Egypt.

When the caravan was nearing Egypt, they met another caravan of traders coming out of

Egypt. They inquired about the business circumstances in Egypt; they found out during the course of their discussion that the merchandises, which Musaddif and his Companions had brought, were not available and scarce in Egypt as well as in great demand.

The merchants, hearing this good news, decided not to sell their goods not less than one hundred percent profit. They arrived in Egypt; the situation didn't differ. It was the same as they have been informed. As agreed previously, they created a black market and did not sell the goods. They doubled the cost and then sold the goods.

Musaddif returned to Madinah with a net profit of one thousand Dinars. He went happily and gladly to Imam al-Sadiq and put before him two bags, each containing one thousand Dinars.

The Imam asked: "What is this?"

He said: "One of the two bags is the capital which you gave me, and the other one – which is equal to the capital – is the net profit which is gained."

The Imam said: "The profit is too high; tell me how did you gain so much profit?!"

The servant replied: "In fact, when we came to understand that the goods became scarce there, we pledged our words not to sell our goods not less than a hundred percent profit of the capital and we did the same!

Imam al-Sadiq said: "Glory be to Allah! Did you do such a work?! Did you swear to create a black market among the Muslims?! Did you swear to sell the goods not less than the net profit equal to the capital?! No! No! No! I do not want such a business and such a profit."

Then the Imam picked up one of the bags and said: "This is my capital", and he did not touch the other bag and said: "I have nothing to do with the other one."

Then he added: "O Musaddif! To sword is easier than to do business lawfully."

Source: Murtada Mutahhari, THE NARRATIVES OF THE VERACIOUS, Story 31.

Financial Lessons of the Story:

1. Looking for livelihood for one's family in order not to depend on others is a form of worship (*'ibadah*).

2. Investing in lawful things that would further earn income.

3. Moral principles must always guide the types of business one engages.

****

STORY 9
THE LATE-COMER OF CARAVAN

In the darkness of night, from a very far distance, they heard a voice of a young man screaming. He was imploring and demanding help. His weak and scrawny camel had remained behind the caravan and lagged entirely. He finally, exhausted, stretched out and slept. He did what he could for moving his camel, but it was in vain. Helplessly standing beside the camel, he was yelling for help.

Meanwhile, the Holy Prophet, who usually moved behind – in the end of the caravan so that a weak and helpless person who parted from the caravan, would not remain alone or helpless – heard the yelling voice of the young man. As the Prophet approached him, he asked: "Who are you?"

"I am Jabir."

"Why were you kept waiting and wondering?"

"O Messenger of Allah! The only reason was that my camel got exhausted."

"Did you have a walking stick?"

"Yes."

"Give it to me."

The Holy Prophet took the stick and with its help made the camel move forward and kneel. Then he made his hands a stirrup and said to Jabir to "mount his camel."

Jabir mounted the camel, and they made their way together while Jabir's camel moved faster. Throughout the way, the Holy Prophet did not stop showing his kindness towards Jabir, whereas Jabir counted and realized that the Holy Prophet had prayed twenty-five times for the remission of his sins.

On the way, the Prophet asked Jabir: "How many children have been left from your father, 'Abd Allah?"

"Seven girls and a boy, myself."

"Has your father left any debts?"

"Yes."

"Well, when you return to Madinah, make an arrangement with the creditors, and at the plucking season of the dates, inform me!"

"All right."

"Did you marry?"

"Yes."

"To whom?"

"To Mrs. so-and-so, daughter of so-and-so, one of the widows of Madinah."

"Why didn't you marry to a young girl of your age?"

"O Messenger of Allah, having so many young and inexperienced sisters, I didn't marry to a young inexperienced woman. I preferred to choose a mature woman for marriage."

"You did your best. How much did you buy this camel?"

"Five ounces of gold."

"I'll purchase it from you at this price. When you arrive in Madinah, come and take the money from me!"

The journey came to an end, and they arrived in Madinah. Jabir brought the camel to submit to the Holy Prophet. He ordered Bilal to give Jabir five ounces of gold for the price of his camel, and in addition to that, three ounces more so that he may pay the debts of his father, 'Abd Allah. He also returned back his camel.

Then the Prophet asked Jabir: "Did you make a contract with the creditors?"

Jabir: "No, O Messenger of Allah!"

"What your father has left is enough for his debts?"

"No, O Messenger of Allah!"

"Inform me at the plucking season of the dates!"

The season of harvest arrived. He informed the Messenger of Allah. The Holy Prophet came and settled all the debts and left enough for Jabir's family.

Source: Murtada Mutahhari, THE NARRATIVES OF THE VERACIOUS, Story 34.

Financial Lessons of the Story:

1. The need to settle one's debt.

2. Preservation of one's self-esteem and personal integrity. Instead of just paying Jabir's debt which will negatively affect his self-esteem, the Holy Prophet bought some items (camel and date fruits) from him so that he could settle his debt out of that money.

3. Utilization of one's energy and talent to earn for a living.

3. To be self-reliant and not to rely on others even for a small thing.

4. Looking for livelihood for one's family in order not to depend on others is a form of worship (*'ibadah*).

5. The Leader is supposed to serve as a model by helping his follower to settle his debt.

****

STORY 10
THE MAN WHO DESIRED GOLD

He grazed sadly at his simple home and the open workshop in which stood a partially completed chariot.

His wife frequently appeared at the door. Her cautious glances in his direction reminded him that the meal bag was almost empty, and he should be at work."

Bansir, the chariot builder, was too engrossed in his own problem to be bothered by the noise of industry within the walls of Babylon. The city was a mix of grandeur and squalor – incredible displays of wealth and the direst poverty. Bansir could not understand why he worked so hard and was still numbered among the lowly.

He was so caught up with his deliberations that he was not aware of his friend Kobbi walking towards him playing his lyre. Kobbi's elaborate salute went unnoticed, must less his request for 'two humble shekels'! (Shekel is an ancient coin.)

"If I did have two shekels," Bansir responded miserably, "to no one could I lend them – not even to you, my best of friends; for they would be my fortune – my entire fortune. No one lends his entire fortune, not even to his best friends."

Shocked, Kobbi listened to Bansir recall his daydream. Bansir dreamed he was a man of means and enjoyed the glorious feeling of contentment and surplus gold flowing from his purse.

"...so why should such pleasant feelings as it aroused turn you into a depressed statue on the wall?" Said Kobbi. "Why indeed! Because when I awoke and remembered how empty was my purse, a feeling of rebellion swept over me." Let us talk it over together...

Recalling their days as young men, Bansir and Kobbi touched on their experiences with money. They had earned so much gold over the years but did not have anything to show for it.

They both had hoped that one day, prosperity would be bestowed upon them! They were coming to the realization that such a blessing was not imminent, often planning and scheming that their families didn't go hungry. Bansir's dismal mood soon caught hold with Kobbi, both of them entirely miserable reaching their threshold and coming up with their best idea yet!

"We do not wish to go on year after year living slavish lives. Working, working, working! Getting nowhere. Might we not find out how others acquire gold and do as they do?" Kobbi inquired.

"Perhaps there is some secret we might learn if we sought from those who knew," replied Bansir thoughtfully.

They remembered a friend, Arkad, who was once their schoolmates and who was 'blessed with prosperity,' and the city claimed to be 'The Richest Man in Babylon'. They decided to consult Arkad.

"You made me realize the reason why we have never found any measure of wealth. We never sought it! In those things toward which we exerted our best endeavors we succeeded. It bids us to learn more that we may prosper more. With a new understanding we shall find more honorable ways to accomplish our desires. Let us go to Arkad this very day," Bansir urged.

Bansir and Kobbi proceeded to gather a group of boyhood friends who had need of the same guidance.

Source: George S. Clason, THE RICHEST MAN IN BABYLON, Chapter 1.

Financial Lessons of the Story:

1. It is not enough to work hard; instead, it is more important to work smart.

2. To work in line with your passion and talent is one thing; how to maximize your profits out of it is another.

3. The amount of income one gets is immaterial if there is no discipline in spending.

4. The importance of seeking for a mentor.

****

THE RICHEST MAN IN BABYLON

Arkad was famous across the land for his great wealth, liberality, and generosity with family and charity. The group that Bansir and Kobbi had assembled opened up their discussion with some interesting perceptions about life.

"Why then should a fickle fate single you out to enjoy all the good things of life and ignore us who are equally deserving?"

"If you have not acquired more than a bare existence in the years since we were youths, it is because you have either failed to learn the laws that govern the building of wealth, or else you do not observe them. 'Fickle fate' is a vicious goddess who brings no permanent good to anyone... makes wanton spenders, who soon dissipate all they receive."

(Easy money doesn't stick around is what Arkad preaches. So true. Think of people close to you who have won lotteries and the like. The fair majority are without today!)

Arkad was asked the obvious question about how he has acquired his fortune. He made an assessment from his early years that the things that brought happiness and contentment were magnified by the existence of wealth.

"Wealth is power. With wealth many things are possible."

When he had this realization, he decided to claim his share of the good things of life because he would not be satisfied with the lot of a poor man. He determined the following:

1. He would hove to immerse himself and study wealth accumulation.

2. Once learned, he would follow the laws and do it well.

Arkad explained to the group that there were two types of learning. One was the things we learned and knew; the other the training that taught us how to find out what we don't know.

Arkad found employment as a scribe and labored for many months without anything to show for it. One of Arkad's clients, a wealthy man called Algamish, wanted a job done overnight. Arkad in exchange for such prompt service requested Algamish to inform him as to how he may too become wealthy.

The first piece of advice from Algamish – "I found the road to wealth when I decided that a part of all I earned was mine to keep." The advice to save no less than a tenth of what Arkad earned was the start of a transformation. "Every gold piece that you save is a slave to work for you. Every copper it earns is its child that also can earn for you."

When Arkad met up with Algamish twelve months later, he had saved a tenth of his earnings but had given it to Azmur the Bricklayer to invest in rare jewels. This was where Algamish's next piece of advice was to make a change for Arkad.

"Every fool must learn," he growled, "but why trust the knowledge of a Brickmaker about jewels?" …"next time if you would have advice about jewels, go to the jewel merchant." "Advice is one thing that is freely given away, but watch that you take only what is worth having."

The jewels the Brickmaker bought were worthless and Arkad learned the lesson. The habit to save was now fully entrenched so he quickly amassed more gold. After another twelve months, Algamish returned to meet with Arkad. Arkad reported that he had been loaning his savings to Agger to Shildmaker who was paying interest on the borrowings. Some of his gold he has using for feasts and buying luxurious items. Algamish advised further:

"You do eat the children of your savings. Then how do you expect them to work for you? And how can they have children that will also work for you? First get an army of golden slaves and then many a rich banquet may you enjoy without regret."

Another 24 months passed and Algamish complimented Arkad on his rigid adherence to his teachings.

"Arkad," he continued, "you have learned the lessons well. You first learned to live on less than you earn. Next you have learned to seek advice from those who were competent... and lastly, you have learned to make gold work for you."

Arkad had learned how to acquire money, how to keep it and how to use it. Algamish made Arkad an offer he couldn't refuse – to work with him and share in his estate. One of the group members Arkad was addressing commented that he was fortunate to be made an heir. Arkad replied, "Fortunate only in that I had the desire to prosper before I first met him."

"Opportunity is a haughty goddess who wastes no time with those who are unprepared."

"Willpower is but the unflinching purpose to carry a task you set for yourself to fulfillment."

"When I set a task for myself, I complete it. Therefore, I am careful not to start difficult and impractical tasks, because I love leisure."

"Wealth grows wherever men exert energy."

Arkad explains that you must live with the thought that:

"A part of all I earn is mine to keep."

"Think about it morning, noon, and night."

"Impress yourself with the idea. Fill yourself with the thought."

"As it grows it will stimulate you."

"Make gold be your slave."

"Seek wise counsel."

The group thanked Arkad for the discussion and dispersed – some silent and still not understanding, sarcastically thinking that Arkad should divide his massive fortune with them!

Others walked away with a new light in their eyes and frequently counseled with Arkad who gave freely of his wisdom.

Source: George S. Clason, THE RICHEST MAN IN BABYLON, Chapter 2.

Financial Lessons of the Story:
1. The amount of income one gets is immaterial if there is no discipline in spending.

2. Wealth is a means, not an end.

3. Investing in things that would further earn income.

4. Maintenance of one's network of friends, co-workers, and relatives.

5. How much you save is not that important, but rather the cultivation of the habit of saving.

6. It is not enough that extra money is saved; it must be invested as well; in other words, apart from setting it aside, it must be allowed to work in order to multiply.

7. The importance of seeking for a mentor and the right mentor at that.

8. The burning desire to be financially independent is the beginning of financial independence.

9. To live on less than you earn.

Story 11

****

53

STORY 12
SEVEN CURES FOR A LEAN PURSE

Good King Sargon was lamenting the economic condition of the city. The rich were getting richer and poor poorer. All of the gold of the city has found its way into the hands of "a few very rich men of our city".

"Why should so few men be able to acquire all the gold?" said the King.

"Because they know how," replied the Chancellor. "One may not condemn a man for succeeding because he knows how."

"Who knows best in all our city how to become wealthy, Chancellor?" asked the King.

"Your question answers for itself, your majesty."

"Who has amassed the greatest wealth in Babylon?"

"Arkad," replied the Chancellor.

Arkad was invited to appear before the King. The start of the conversation sums up the topic.

"How did you become wealthy? You had nothing to start with?" asked the King.

"Only a great desire for wealth. Besides this, nothing," Arkad replied.

"Is there any secret to acquiring wealth? Can it be taught?" asked the King.

"It is practical, your majesty. That which one man knows can be taught to others," said Arkad.

The King wished for the knowledge that Arkad had accrued to be shared with the city folk. The King selected the 'Chosen Hundred' to sit with Arkad. The great man stood before the hundred and explained how he had nothing as a youth other than am empty purse. He sought every remedy for a lean purse and found seven. The Seven Cures for a Lean Curse:

1. Start your purse to fattening

"For every ten coins you place within your purse, take out for use but nine. Your purse will start to fatten at once and its increasing weight will feel good in your hand and bring satisfaction to your soul."

2. Control your expenditures

"Budget your expenses that you may have coins to pay for your necessities, to pay for your enjoyments and to gratify your worthwhile desires without spending more than nine-tenths of your earnings."

3. Make your gold multiply

"Put each coin to laboring that it may reproduce its kind even as flocks of the field and help to bring to you income, a stream of wealth that shall flow constantly into your purse.

4. Guard your treasures from loss

"Guard your treasure from loss by investing only where your principle is safe, where it may be reclaimed if desirable, and where you will not fail to collect a fair rental. Consult with wise men. Secure the advice of those experienced in the profitable handling of gold. Let their wisdom protect your treasure from unsafe investments."

5. Make your dwelling a profitable investment

"Own your own home."

6. Insure a future income

"Provide for in advance for the needs of your growing age and the protection of your family."

7. Increase your ability to earn

"Cultivate your own powers, to study and become wiser, to become more skillful, to act as to respect yourself."

Arkad ended his lecture urging the hundred that there is more gold than you can dream of, abundance for all, so go forth "grow wealthy, as it is your right."

Source: Goerge S. Clason, THE RICHEST MAN IN BABYLON, Chapter 3.

Financial Lessons of the Story:

1. Utilization of one's energy and talent to earn for a living.

2. The amount of income one gets is immaterial if there is no discipline in spending.

3. It is not enough that extra money is saved; it must be invested as well; in other words, apart from setting it aside, it must be allowed to work in order to multiply.

4. To look for ways to protect or insure one's assets and income.

5. Make your house a profitable investment.

6. The greatest investment is investment in one's own self – how to make yourself more productive and profitable.

7. There are many opportunities to earn, and you just need to explore and discover them.

****

ABOUT THE EDITOR

Mansoor Limba is a writer, translator, university professor, chess trainer, and blogger. He is a PhD holder in International Relations and BA holder in Islamic Studies who writes and translates books (Persian into English and Filipino, English into Filipino) on such subjects as international politics, history, political philosophy, Islamic finance, jurisprudence (*fiqh*), scholastic theology (*'ilm al-kalam*), Qur'anic sciences, hadith, ethics, and mysticism. Have an experience with his multidisciplinary taste by visiting his blog at https://mlimba.com and financial literary advocacy at https://muslimandmoney.com and buying his books at https://www.elzistyle.com.

OTHER BOOKS BY MANSOOR LIMBA

Please visit your favorite ebook retailer to discover other books by Mansoor Limba:

Written Works
The Power of International Quds Day in the Cyberspace
My Tehran Diary
Light Moments in Vienna
Muslim Couple and Money: 8 Practical Financial Tips for
    Newlywed Muslim Couples
12 Financial Stories for Muslim Kids
Muslim and Debt: 5 Practical Steps to Freedom from Debt
Kabuntalan through the Centuries: A Narrative of History and
    Culture
The Hermeneutics of Violent Extremism in Mindanao
Mutahhari is Mutahhari: The Making of a Thinker

Translation Works
Imam Khomeini, Ethics and Politics
Freedom: The Unstated Facts and Points
Imam Khomeini and the Muslim World
Sahifeh-ye Imam: An Anthology of Imam Khomeini's Speeches,
    Messages, Interviews, Decrees, Religious Permissions and
    Letters (Volume 20)
Sahifeh-ye Imam: An Anthology of Imam Khomeini's Speeches,
    Messages, Interviews, Decrees, Religious Permissions and
    Letters (Volume 21)
An Overview of the Mahdi's Government
The Radiance of the Secrets of Prayer
The Qur'an as Reflected in *Nahj al-Balaghah*
In the Presence of the Beloved: Commentaries on *Du'a' al-*
    Iftitah, Du'a' Abu Hamzah al-Thumali and *Du'a' Makarim al-*
    Akhlaq
A Commentary on Prayer
A Cursory Glance at the Theory of *Wilayat al-Faqih*

Training and Education in Islam

The Theory of Knowledge: An Islamic Perspective

Islamic Political Theory, Volume 1 (Legislation)

Islamic Political Theory, Volume 2 (Statecraft)

Investigations and Challenges: Discourses on Current Cultural, Sociopolitical and Religious Issues

An Introduction to *Hadith*: History and Sources

Introduction to the Sciences of the Qur'an, Volume 1

Introduction to the Sciences of the Qur'an, Volume 2

Discursive Theology, Volume 1

Discursive Theology, Volume 2

Philosophy of Religion

Fitrah: Man's Natural Disposition

Philosophy of Ethics

Hijab and Mental Health

Risalah Liqa' Allah: A Treatise on the Stages of Mystical Wayfaring toward the Station of Beatific Vision

The Revival of Islamic Thought

Risalah Ma'rifat Allah: An Exposition of Imam 'Ali ibn Musa al-Rida's ('a) Sermon on the Gnosis of Allah

Misbah al-Shari'ah: A Commentary on *Misbah al-Shari'ah* (Lantern of the Path) Attributed to Imam Ja'far al-Sadiq (*'a*)

Esoteric Traditions: An Exposition of Imam Musa ibn Ja'far's (*'a*) Mystical and Philosophical Traditions

Imam al-Rida's (*'a*) Esoteric Traditions: An Exposition of Selected Traditions from *'Uyun Akhbar al-Rida*

Risalah Sayr wa Suluk: An Exposition of Sayyid Bahr al-'Ulum's Treatise on Mystical Wayfaring

Scientific Approach in Translating and Interpreting the Noble Qur'an and Traditions

Tafsir-e Rushan: An Elucidated Exegesis of the Qur'an, Volume 1

The Issue of Ḥijāb

Replies to Critiques of the Book 'The Issue of Ḥijāb'

CONNECT WITH MANSOOR LIMBA

I really appreciate you reading my book! Here are my social media coordinates:

Add me on Facebook: http://facebook.com/mansoor.limba

Follow me on Twitter: http://twitter.com/mansoor_limba

Follow me on Instagram: https://www.instagram.com/m_limba

Pin my photos: https://www.pinterest.ph/mansoorlimba

Favorite my Smashwords author page: https://www.smashwords.com/profile/view/mlimba

Favorite my Amazon author page: www.amazon.com/author/mansoorlimba

Connect on LinkedIn: https://ph.linkedin.com/pub/mansoor-limba/b6/383/720

Subscribe to my blog: http://www.mlimba.com

Subscribe to my channel: http://www.youtube.com/c/wayfaringwithmansoor

Visit my financial literacy website: https://www.muslimandmoney.com

Purchase my books: https://www.elzistyle.com